Water Beetles

Dorothy Childs Hogner

Illustrated by Nils Hogner

Water
Beetles

Thomas Y. Crowell Company / New York

By the Author Butterflies • Earthworms
Frogs and Polliwogs • Grasshoppers and Crickets
Snails • Spiders • Water Beetles

The author wishes to thank Mr. John C. Pallister, Research Associate, Department of Entomology, and Miss Alice Gray, Scientific Assistant, both of the American Museum of Natural History for their helpful suggestions.

Contents

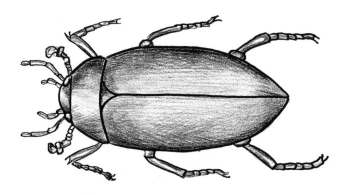

The world is very full of beetles, it would seem. Beetles make up forty per cent of all the species of insects in the whole world. Scientists now know of over a quarter of a million different species.

Beetles live in all sorts of places. Some beetles live under the bark of trees. Others, such as the June bug—which is called a bug but is a true beetle—are at home on the ground and in the air. So, too, are the lightning "bugs," which are beetles.

Water beetles are another large and interesting group of insects.

Water beetles are found in fresh-water pools. Most of them are at home in still waters. Some species live in running streams. One kind lives in wet sand, on the banks of rivers and lakes. Another very, very rare beetle lives in cracks in rocks, on the coast by the sea, where the high tides flood over it.

A Water Beetle on the Outside

Water beetles, like land beetles, have six jointed legs, and, usually, two pairs of wings.

You can see the skeleton of a water beetle without looking inside the insect. The skeleton, like that of other insects, is on the outside of its body. The heart and other inside organs are covered by a cylinder that forms the skeleton.

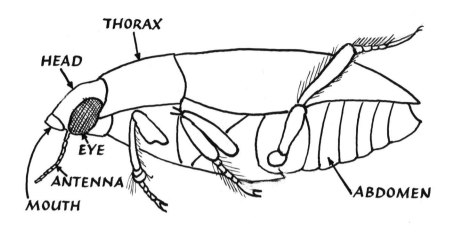

THORAX
HEAD
EYE
ANTENNA
MOUTH
ABDOMEN

The skeleton is made of chitin, a horny material. The body can bend because there are flexible grooves in the body wall.

The three main body parts are the head, the middle or thorax, and the abdomen.

On the head of a water beetle are its antennae (the feelers), the mouth, and the eyes. The feelers are jointed, and so the beetle can bend them.

The feelers of some water beetles are clublike.

Others are slender and threadlike. A water beetle uses its feelers to help find its way. With its feelers it explores leaves and other things.

The mouth of a water beetle is made for chewing. The jaws are strong. Some water beetles have a groove in their jaws, through which they may suck blood from their prey. The palps on the lips are also used for feeling things.

A beetle's eyes are compound. This means that, unlike our eyes, which are simple, they are made up of hundreds of tiny, six-sided eyes. Each little eye helps a beetle to see objects all around it.

The middle part, the thorax, is itself made up of three parts, and each part is made up of several plates. The plates on the thorax of different beetles are of different shapes, and in different positions. These plates help scientists tell one beetle from another.

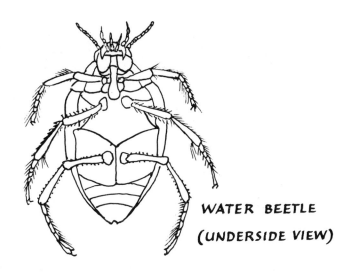

WATER BEETLE
(UNDERSIDE VIEW)

On each one of the three parts of the thorax is one pair of legs, making six legs in all. The hind legs of many water beetles are flattened and fringed with hair. They are used like oars, for swimming.

The wings of a water beetle are on the thorax. Only the two hind wings are used in flight. They are on the third part of the thorax. They are thin, and usually longer than the front wings. When

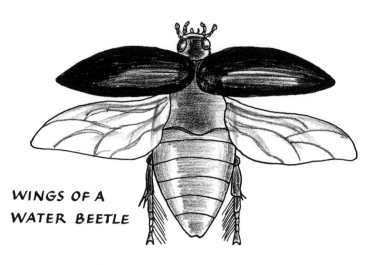

WINGS OF A WATER BEETLE

not in use, the hind wings lie folded under the front wings.

The two front wings are attached to the second part of the thorax. They are thick and hard. When the beetle is in flight, the front wings are held out at the sides and act like the wings of an airplane. When the insect is not in flight, the front wings act as a cover for the delicate hind wings. When at rest, the front wings meet in a straight line down the back.

6

Scientists call beetles the sheath-wing insects. The front wings are the sheath wings. A sheath means a cover, such as a case for a sword.

The third part of the body, the abdomen, is usually made up of ten ringed parts. Some of the rings are hidden under the wings on the back. These ringed parts cover inside organs.

There are no legs or wings on the abdomen.

A water beetle does not have a nose such as we have. It breathes through tiny holes called spiracles. These breathing holes are in the body wall.

Many water beetles can make faint sounds in the air and under water. But they have no voice chords in their throats. Some make noises by rubbing their hind legs on the underside of the abdomen, the third part of the body. Others rub the rings of the abdomen upon the under part of the front wings.

Some water beetles can stay under water for a very long time. They have no gills like a fish. Why, then, do they not drown? You and I would, unless, like a skin diver, we took our air down under with us.

This is just what a water beetle does. It goes to the surface of the water and traps an air bubble under its hind wings, or under its body. Then down it goes, with a pocket full of oxygen right over the places where its breathing holes are.

These beetles can stay under water a long time.

A Water Beetle on the Inside

Down the center of a water beetle's body is a canal. It is open at both ends. The front opening is the mouth. Behind the mouth is a kind of throat, called the pharynx. Next comes the gullet, then the stomach. Behind the stomach are the intestines. The hind opening is the anus. Food taken in at the mouth goes down the canal. On the way, it is digested. The wastes go out the tail end, the anus.

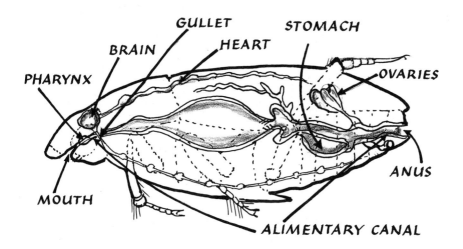

Above the canal, and under the back, is the beetle's heart, a long tube.

The brain of a water beetle, like ours, is in its

head. A beetle also has small nerve centers in each segment which serve as small brains.

We take in air through our noses, to our lungs. A water beetle breathes through tubes. These tubes lead off from the breathing holes and take oxygen to the tissues of the body. Out through these same holes goes the harmful carbon dioxide gas that has formed.

The ovaries, where the eggs form in the mother beetle, and the sex organs of the father beetle, are in the lower abdomen.

A Water Beetle's Birthday

Like a chicken, the water beetle begins life as an egg. And, like a chicken, a mother water beetle lays eggs. But this is the only way a mother water beetle can be compared to a hen.

10

One kind of water beetle makes holes in the surface of underwater leaves, and lays her eggs, one by one, in the tissues of the leaves. Other water beetles make fine cradles for their eggs, spinning silklike, waterproof egg cases. One of these beetles may deposit as many as a hundred eggs in a single case.

Some take their egg cases with them, wherever they go. They hold the little package under their bodies with their hind legs.

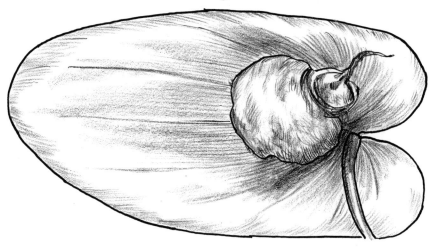

EGG CASE ON UNDERSIDE OF A LEAF

11

Another water beetle fastens her egg case to a floating, underwater leaf, such as a pond lily. This cradle is rocked by the waves.

However, the baby water beetles are not so safe in these egg cases as one might think. When the baby beetles come out of the eggs, but are still in the case, they start eating each other. They are cannibals.

Those babies that do live, and leave the egg case, have no nurse. The mother takes no care of them. She might not know her own children, they look so different from her.

The larva, as the young of a water beetle is called, is long and wormlike. It has six legs, just like its parents. But it has no wings. Its body is made up of a number of ringed parts, and a head.

Some of the young of water beetles, like their parents, breathe air.

Other water beetle larvae have gills. They breathe under water, somewhat as fishes do. The gills of the young of water beetles are on the sides. They look like a fringe.

The New Look

When full grown, the larva of a water beetle is ready to take the third step in its life. The first step was the egg. The second was the larva. The third is the pupa, the form in which the larva rests while it takes on the shape of an adult beetle. The pupa is a kind of case.

The young of most water beetles change into beetles in late summer, or in the fall of the year. When the time comes, the larva stops eating. It crawls out of the water, onto the shore.

Some burrow down into the earth. These make a pupa for themselves in a round cell, underground.

Other water beetle larvae, when they change into pupae, first make a covering of bits of earth and leaves. They attach themselves to blades of grass or other plants.

Once the larva has changed into a pupa it stays quietly in place. But great changes are going on within the pupa. The body shortens and widens. Wings form. A larva which has gills loses these

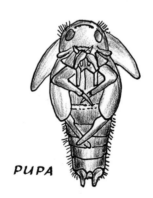

PUPA

gills. The hard beetle body replaces the soft ringed body of the young.

In about three weeks to a month, the adult beetle is ready to come out. Many do come out at once. If, however, the time of year is late fall, the beetles may remain in the quiet state, inside their pupae, until spring.

When the beetles come out, they go back into the water and look hungrily around for something to eat. They attack insects which live in water, such as caddis worms. They eat snails, as well as winged insects which fall into their pool.

Water Beetle Families

Some beetles are so rare you will probably never see them. Others are common.

There are more than a dozen families of water

15

beetles in the United States. In this case a family does not mean a mother and father beetle with their children. It means a group of beetles which are, in many ways, alike.

Members of each family are quite like each other. But they differ in size and markings. Some members of a family are small. Others in the same family may be medium-sized. Still others are large.

Some members of a family may have smooth heads. Others in the same family may have furrows on their heads. Some may be solid-colored while others have different-colored markings.

In general, water beetles range in size from less than an eighth of an inch to a little more than an inch and a half in length. This means that one may be about as tiny as a flea while another may be as big as a baby turtle.

Scientists can tell water beetles apart by:

the shape and the placing of the plates on their
   middle part, the thorax;
the size and color of the body;
the form of the feelers;
and the shape and looks of other outside body
   parts.

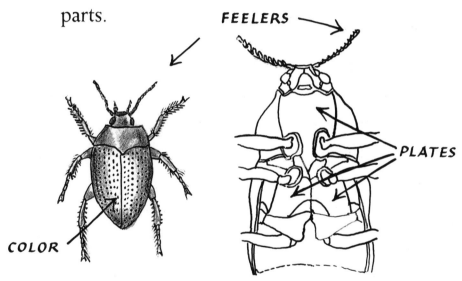

Anyone who wishes to tell them apart in the
field should learn their habits. This is the easiest

way to identify water beetles, because members of different water beetle families behave in quite different ways.

Whirligigs

Whirligigs whirl around and around each other on the surface of a still pool, or a slowly moving stream. They leave a beautiful pattern of widening ripples in their wake. They may suddenly stop and rest all together, for the whirligigs are social. They like to go about with each other. Sometimes there may be more than a hundred on one small pool.

Whirligig beetles are little beetles. They range in size from under a quarter of an inch to five-eighths of an inch in length. They are oval in form.

WHIRLIGIGS

19

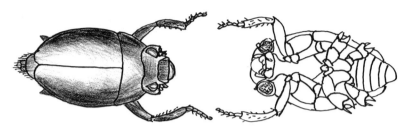

WHIRLIGIG AND UNDERSIDE VIEW

At first glance, one of these beetles looks as though it had four eyes. Not so. Like other beetles, a whirligig has only two eyes. But the sharp edge of the head divides each of a whirligig's eyes. Thus one half of each eye looks at the sky, and the other half looks down into the pool. So it seems to be a four-eyed beetle.

The whirligigs have quite long front legs. The hind legs, which are the swimming legs, are short, much flattened, and fringed with hair. These legs are their oars.

The underbody of a whirligig is covered with short hairs. These hairs trap a film of air which

20

makes a cushion under them. It helps to hold up the beetles on the surface of the water, as they go whirling around. They do not, as many water beetles do, use this trapped air for breathing.

They do not dive unless frightened. They can, however, swim under water very well.

These lively little beetles feed mostly upon small insects that fall into the water. When a fly strikes the surface of their pool, the whirligigs swim madly around and around it. They keep hold of the fly and tear off bits to eat as they swim.

The mother whirligig lays her eggs on the underside of lily pads and other water-plant leaves.

The young of a whirligig beetle has two hooks on the end of its abdomen. With the help of these hooks, it propels itself forward and backward, over the bottom of the pool.

The whirligig larva does not have to come to

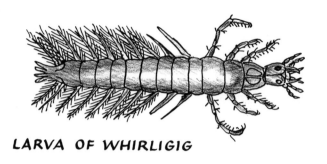

LARVA OF WHIRLIGIG

the surface of the water for air. It has gills. Eight long, fringed gills are attached to either side of the abdomen at the location of the breathing holes. With these gills it breathes under water.

The gills make the whirligig larva look like a little centipede.

Diving Beetles

This family of water beetles is called the predaceous diving beetle. The name gives the key to their habits: they are great divers and they are predaceous, which means that they feed on living creatures. They attack and devour insects, snails, and even small fish.

The divers are the biggest family of water beetles. Some of the members are small in size. They measure under a quarter-inch in length. Others are among the largest beetles found in water in the United States. These giants measure an inch and a half in length.

They are handsome insects, with shining brown-black bodies. Some of them are lightly marked with yellow. They all have slender, threadlike feelers.

The best way to tell a diving beetle from other water beetles is to watch one in action. Creep up noiselessly to the bank of a still pool. See if you can spot an upside-down beetle. If you do, it is a predaceous diving beetle. A diving beetle rests with its tail at the surface of the water. Its body

floats under water, at a downward angle. It also
hangs in this position to take on air.

When taking on air, the diver raises its wing
covers (front wings) and traps a little air bubble
underneath these wings. Then down it goes in a
flash.

And watch the diver swim. It moves its hind
legs together, forward and back, as you move a
pair of oars when rowing a boat.

Just this movement of its legs, at the same stroke, is enough to tell the difference between the diving beetle and another water beetle which, at first glance, looks like a diver's twin. (See water scavenger beetle.)

The divers are strong fliers. They often fly from pool to pool. At night they are attracted to lights, so you may see one come flying into your porch after dark.

The young of a diving beetle is called a water tiger. It deserves its name. It is very bloodthirsty.

Like its parents, it feeds on insects and other small water life. It is not afraid of creatures bigger than itself. It is the terror of the woodland pools.

When a water tiger sees a polliwog, for instance, it remains still. It waits until the polliwog is close, then it pounces. It grabs the polliwog with its sicklelike jaws. It holds on and sucks the

polliwog's blood until it has sucked the polliwog
dry.

   Like its parents, the water tiger is an air breather.
It has two breathing tubes at the end of its abdomen. It, too, comes up tail first to the surface of
the pool. It takes on a bubble and down it goes
with an air supply to hunt among the lily pads and
other water plants.

When the water tiger is full grown, it crawls out of the water onto the shore. It burrows down into the ground where it makes a round cell. There it pupates, that is, it changes over into a diving beetle.

A Beetle Garbage Collector

Everyone knows what a garbage collector does. He goes around from house to house and takes away trash in his truck.

Among the water beetles there is a kind of garbage collector. It is called a water scavenger. The name scavenger simply means that this beetle helps keep the water clean. It does not, of course, take away any trash. But it feeds mostly on pond scum, rotting plant life, and dead insects. This results in a natural cleanup. Sometimes, however, it takes live prey.

It is not easy, at first glance, to tell the difference between a member of this beetle family and a member of the diving beetle family. Both are black in color. Both vary in size from small to large. The largest scavenger beetle, however, may measure a little over an inch and a half in length. This makes it the largest water beetle in the United States.

One difference between these look-alike families is in the feelers. While the diving beetle's antennae are slender and threadlike, those of the scavenger are clublike. You do not often see the feelers of the scavenger when it is in the water. It keeps them folded down under the body, except when taking on air. What you usually see are the palps, part of the lips. The palps are used as feelers.

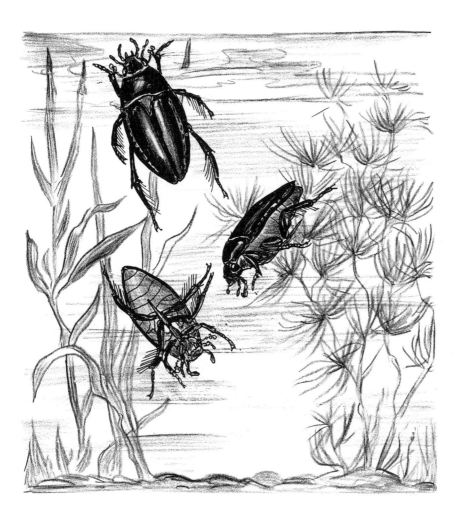

WATER SCAVENGER BEETLE

29

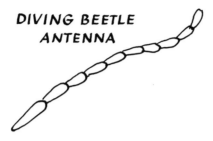

DIVING BEETLE ANTENNA

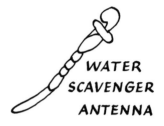

WATER SCAVENGER ANTENNA

The easy way to tell the difference between these beetles is to watch them in action. Watch a beetle swim. The scavenger moves its legs alternately, back and forth, as if it were running. The diver moves its hind legs in one stroke, together.

Another way to tell a scavenger is to watch it take on air. The scavenger beetle rises *head* first to the surface of the water. It reaches forward its feelers and takes on a bubble of air. It spreads the air on the underside of its body. Then down it goes. The diver rises to take on air *tail* first.

The larva of the scavenger beetle is fat and fringed. Several threadlike fringes come from

30

either side of its abdomen. They look like, but are not, gills. The young, like its parents, breathes air. It feeds on small insects and other live prey.

The Long-Horned Leaf Beetle

This is a common member of a large family of leaf beetles. Most of them live on land. The long-horned leaf beetle, however, loves the water. It is seldom seen far from a pool. It is a small, slender beetle, not more than a half-inch in length. It is easy to see. Its body shines like metal: purple, green, or bronze.

The long feelers have given it the name long-horned. It waves its "horns" about and in front of itself. Thus it feels its way across a lily pad and other water-plant leaves.

31

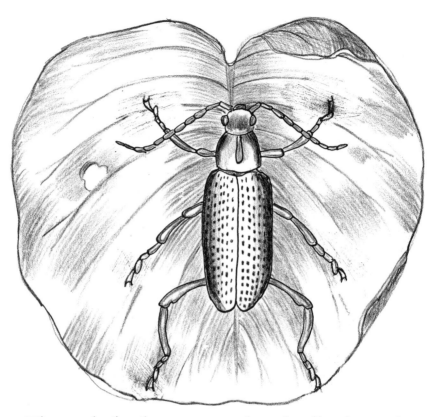

The underbody is covered with silky hairs that keep it dry in water.

The long-horned leaf beetle is a good, strong flier. It often takes to the air.

Small holes in pond lily pads are a sign that

LONG-HORNED LEAF BEETLE LARVA

these beetles are around. When ready to lay her eggs, the mother long-horned leaf beetle cuts a small hole in a pond lily leaf. She then puts the end of her abdomen into the hole. She lays two rows of eggs, in a crescent, on the underside of the leaf.

The young hatch from these eggs in about ten days. The larvae live under water, even though they have no gills. They feed, under water, on the stems of water plants. They also bore into the stems of these plants and take air from the stems.

When full grown, the larva makes a watertight

33

cocoon. It takes a supply of air from the plant stems into this cocoon. When the larva has changed into a beetle, some of the air makes a film on the hairs of its underbody. This gives the new beetle air to breathe while it floats up to the surface of the pool.

Riffle Beetles

Look for these beetles, not in still pools, but in riffles in streams. They are among the few beetles that like fast running water. That is why they are called riffle beetles.

They are small, black beetles, the biggest being about a quarter of an inch long. They have extra-long toes on their front legs, which is why they are sometimes called long-toed water beetles.

More often the riffle beetles are called water-penny beetles. The name "water-penny" comes from the form of their young. The larvae are almost round, very flat, and copper-colored. You will find them clinging tightly to the underside of stones in rapid flowing water. They look like part of the stone itself. Turn one over, and you will see that it has legs and gills.

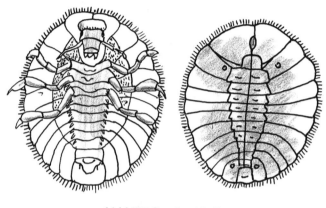

WATER-PENNY

Crawling Water Beetles

The crawling water beetles are very small. The biggest is no more than a fifth of an inch in length. They are oval in shape, and brown in color, spotted with yellow.

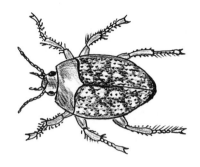

CRAWLING
WATER BEETLE
(ENLARGED)

Crawling water beetles are very common. They move slowly about in masses of vegetation, at or near the surface of a pool. They are also found among trash on the bottom.

They feed on algae–pond scum.

The larva of one of the crawling water beetles is an air breather.

The larva of another crawling water beetle has gills which look like long spines on the sides of its body. It does not have to come up for air.

The young eat the same food as their parents, pond scum.

37

Round Sand Beetles

This is a family of small, oval beetles, with rounded backs. They live in wet sand on the shores of rivers and lakes. They may be seen running over the wet sand, or burrowing into it. Sometimes they run over water.

Both the beetles and their young eat small insects.

ROUND
SAND BEETLE

The Rice Water Weevil

A weevil is a beetle with a snout. The feelers of a weevil are part way down its snout.

Most weevils are land beetles, but several like water.

The rice water weevil is a small, brownish bee-

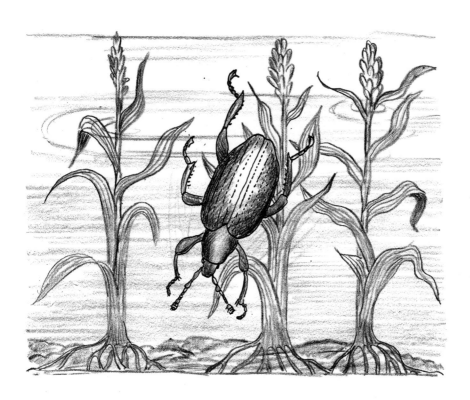

tle. It swims under and on the surface of water. It feeds on the leaves of water plants that grow above the surface. It is called the rice weevil because it often feeds on the leaves of rice plants.

The young of the rice weevil feeds on the roots of rice and other water plants.

A Rare River Beetle

Look for this rare beetle in fast-running, cold mountain streams, in the West of North America, or in faraway Tibet! It is a dark-colored, oval beetle, about five-eighths of an inch long. It is at home among the stones and sunken logs on the bottom of mountain rivers. If knocked off its perch, it tumbles helplessly about in the water, for it cannot swim.

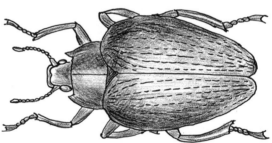

The river beetle can, however, fly. It often flies along the banks of a stream. It also suns itself on rocks above the water level.

The Beaver Beetle

A beaver is a great water animal. It swims and dives, and spends most of its time in water.

The beaver beetle is a parasite. It makes its home on the body of a living beaver. It lives a life much like that of a louse. It has no hind wings. It cannot fly. It cannot swim, either. So it spends its life crawling about on its moving house, a beaver.

The only person who usually sees beaver beetles is the fur trapper. The fur trapper may shake dead beaver beetles off a dried beaver skin before he sends it to market.

Most water beetles do no harm. They live their lives eating and being eaten in pools and rivers. Those which eat pond scum and dead insects are helpful in cleaning up the water.

The rice weevil, however, is a pest in rice fields.

And the water tiger, the larva of the diving beetle, can do a great deal of harm in a fish hatchery. A fish hatchery is a fish farm, where fish are raised. The water tiger feeds on the small fish.

Cousins

The water beetles have thousands and thousands of cousins which live on land. Many of the land beetles are common. Among them are the ladybird beetles, and the potato-bug beetles.

Less common are the big, stout rhinoceros, elephant, and unicorn land beetles.

The unicorn beetle is a greenish-gray beetle, marked with blotches of black. The father unicorn beetle has a horn on its head. The unicorn

UNICORN BEETLE

beetle living in the South measures up to two and one-half inches long.

The giant of all the beetles in the United States, either in water or on land, is the unicorn beetle of Arizona. It is a little over two and a half inches in length.

Beetle Watching

It is fun to go water beetle watching. But don't do it unless you are very patient. One may have to lie on one's belly or row about in a boat for hours. Then maybe you will see nothing living but frogs and polliwogs, and overhead, some birds. This does not add to your knowledge of beetles.

The wise place to do beetle watching is at home. For this you must set up an aquarium for water beetles to live in.

An aquarium is a glass container that will hold water.

You may buy a standard-size aquarium, 14 inches long, 8 inches wide, and 10 inches deep, at a tropical fish store. This makes a luxury home for water beetles. You do not need so expensive an

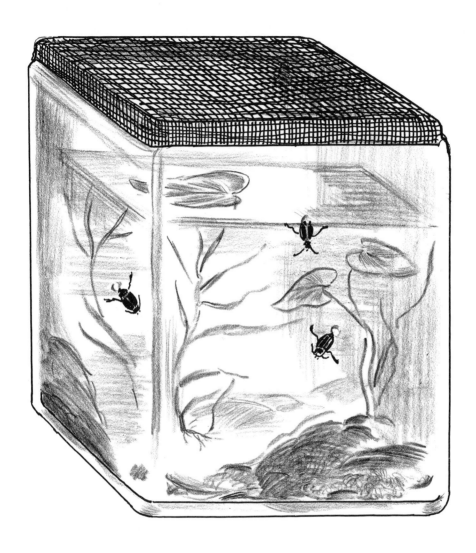

45

aquarium, however. Water beetles will get on just as well in a less fancy home.

A second-hand glass wet-battery jar makes a beautiful aquarium. A wet-battery jar measures 8 inches long, by 6½ inches wide, by 10 inches deep. They are often sold in second-hand shops.

Or you may buy a small glass container at the five and dime store. These containers are usually bought by people who like to raise moss and other land plants.

If you don't want to spend your allowance to buy an aquarium, use a quart Mason jar. One water beetle should live happily for months in a quart Mason jar.

Because most water beetles are good fliers, screen the top of your aquarium. Otherwise your beetles will fly away.

If you want to bring home a live water beetle,

you must have two things: a dip net and a collector's jar.

A dip net is somewhat like a butterfly net, but it is stronger. With a dip net, you go dipping along the bottom of pools. You dip up stones and sticks, as well as beetles. When used this way, a butterfly net would break all to pieces.

To make a dip net, first get a stout pole. An old broom handle would be just fine. Then buy a yard and a half of cheesecloth, 36 inches wide.

Find or buy a stout piece of wire, at least an eighth of an inch thick, and about 50 inches long. Make two small grooves in the broom stick (see picture on page 48).

Form the wire into a circle, and bend over about three inches of each end. Set these bent ends into the grooves in the stick. Tie them tight to the pole with stout twine. Sew the netting

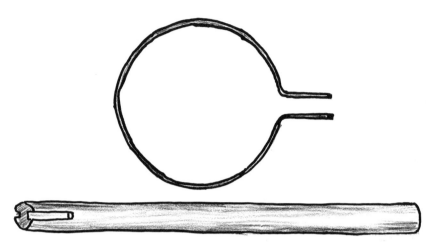

PARTS OF DIP NET

around the wire. Then sew up the side and bottom seam.

For your collector's jar, use a Mason jar with a metal dome lid and band. Remove the lid. Replace the lid with a circle of wire window screen, cut a little bigger than the lid. Screw on the band, to hold the screen in place. Fill the jar with water.

There you are, ready for the field.

Going After Whirligigs

You are lucky. First thing, you spot a swarm of whirligigs, whirling on a pool.

They are easy to see but hard to catch. When you go after them they will glide away, every time.

The best way to catch a whirligig beetle is to hold your net under the surface of the water, *near* to the place where the beetles are whirling. Sit very still. Soon one or several whirligigs are bound to whirl over your net. Then up, *quick*, with the net, and turn the net sidewise, to close the top. Reach into the net with your hand, and remove the beetle gently with your fingers. Put the beetle in your collector's jar.

When you pick up a whirligig beetle, you will notice a fruity odor. When alarmed, whirligigs give off a juice that smells somewhat like apples.

If you see a beetle or a larva coming up for air, or swimming in a pool, net it. But chances are that you will catch more beetles, other than the whirligigs, by blind netting. Go to a small pool, or near shore, in quiet, shallow water in a pond. Pick a spot where water plants grow. Sweep the bottom with your net. Or go out in a boat where the pond lilies grow. Sweep your net among the plants. Then sort the material in your net. This may include polliwogs, small fish, and trash, and, we hope, some beetles.

Warning

If you catch a water scavenger beetle, handle it with care. This beetle has a sharp spine on its un-

derside. It can give you a bad prick on your finger. So, pick up the beetle with your fingers on its sides, *not* on its belly.

Care of the Aquarium

Now you have a beetle or a larva in your collector's jar. Take home, also, some plants for your aquarium. You can buy water plants at stores which sell goldfish and tropical fish. But you can just as well pick them up yourself, where the beetles are.

Good aquarium plants are eel-grass, often called wild celery, water milfoil, and water-weed (Elodea). Also good is the small yellow pond lily. Don't take too many plants. Three or four will do.

Wrap your plants in wet newspaper to keep them damp until you get home.

You will also need some clean sand, and a pretty rock or two.

To plant your aquarium, spread an inch and a half to two inches of sand on the bottom. Add the small rocks. Set the plant roots in the sand. Fill the aquarium to within an inch of the top with water.

What do you feed water beetles? Give them dead flies, grasshoppers, or other insects. They will also thrive on small bits of meat, raw or cooked.

This, of course, is natural food for a scavenger beetle. But even the bloodthirsty diving beetle and its young, the water tiger, will eat this food if they cannot get living prey.

The main thing to remember is, do not feed too much at one time. If you do, the water may become foul with uneaten food. It will then be necessary to change the water.

Get a length of rubber tube about four feet long. You can buy such a tube at the drugstore. Set a pan below the level of the bottom of the aquarium.

Hold one end of the tube under the cold water faucet. When water runs through, pinch both ends of the tube with your fingers. This will hold the tube full of water.

Now hold one end of the tube deep in the water in the aquarium. Hold the other end over the pan. Release your fingers. Water will then start flowing out of the aquarium. This is called siphoning.

53

Watch out that you do not suck up a beetle in the tube. Refill the aquarium at once.

Now to Enjoy

Water beetles keep very active in an aquarium. The little whirligigs go whirling around and around. You would think that they would get dizzy!

The diving beetles are the swiftest. Up one swirls, tail first, to the surface of the water. It takes on air, then down it flashes, with its bubble, to hide behind a water plant.

The most graceful is the young of the diver, the water tiger. To see it swim, who would ever think that it was bloodthirsty? It swims gracefully forward, and as easily backward. Its body bends like

54

a dancer's. It darts quickly. Its thin legs seem to be spinning. Then it stops still. To keep upright in one place under water it flicks a leg or two now and then. It is fascinating to watch. And it looks so dainty, but–it will probably eat any other larvae you put with it.

Do not put the adult diving beetles in an aquarium with their young. In this case, the beetles will very probably eat their children.

Whatever beetles you may catch, you can be sure that you will spend hours watching them. Water beetles are fun to keep and study. So, happy water beetling to you, in the field, and then in your aquarium.

Index

56

About the Author
and Illustrator

Dorothy Childs Hogner is a Connecticut Yankee born in Manhattan. She spent her first year in New York and then the Childs family moved to an old white clapboard house on a hundred-acre farm in Connecticut.

Mrs. Hogner attended Wellesley College and Parsons Art School in New York, and she was graduated from the University of New Mexico. She is the author of many books for children, several of which are illustrated by her husband, Nils Hogner.

Mr. Hogner, who is primarily a mural painter, is an active member of the National Society of Mural Painters and the Architectural League of New York. His "Memorial to the Four Chaplains" may be seen at Temple University in Philadelphia.

The Hogners spend some time in their New York City apartment; but they are usually found at their herb farm in Litchfield, Connecticut, where they raise everything from basil to sweet cicely.